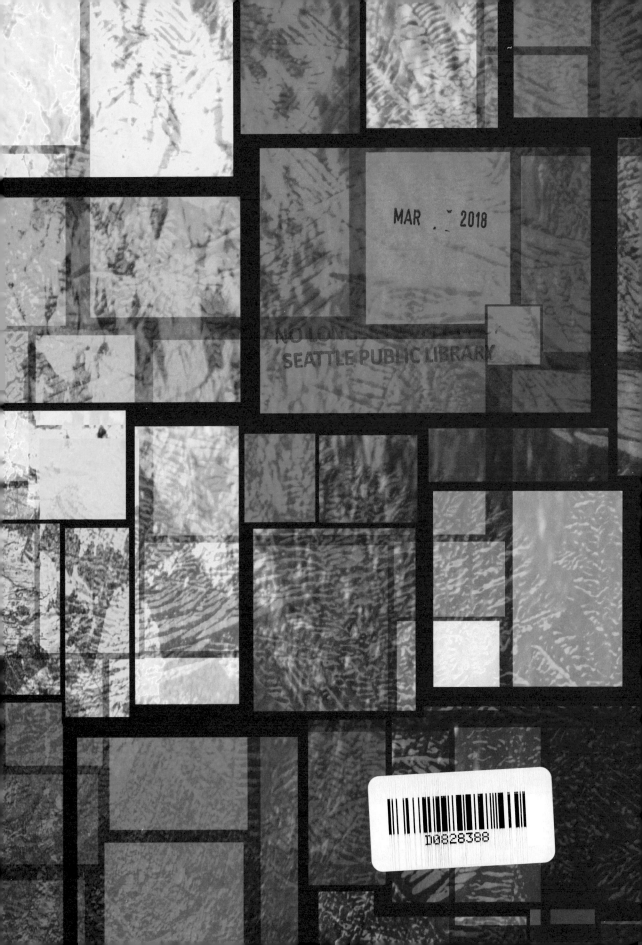

MATH EVERYWHERE

GET IN SHAPE

Two-Dimensional and Three-Dimensional Shapes

Rob Colson

Children's Press®
An Imprint of Scholastic Inc.

Acknowledgments and Photo Credits

Library of Congress Cataloging-in-Publication Data
A CIP catalog record for this book is available from the Library of Congress.

Copyright © The Watts Publishing Group, 2016
First published by Franklin Watts 2016
Published in the United States by Scholastic Inc. 2018

Printed in China

SCHOLASTIC, CHILDREN'S PRESS, and associated logos are trademarks and/or registered trademarks of Scholastic Inc.

1 2 3 4 5 6 7 8 9 10 R 27 26 25 24 23 22 21 20 19 18

Photo credits:
t-top, b-bottom, l-left, r-right, c-center, front cover-fc, back cover-bc
All images courtesy of Dreamstime.com, unless indicated: Inside front Btktan; fc, bc Pablo631; fc, 6b, Dayzeren; 1c, 14t Starserfer; 4b, 21b, 26c Mexrix; 5t Lluecke; 5c Fotyma; 5b Oocoskun; 6c Studioloco; bctr, 8tl Offscreen; 9tr Beho206; 9b Leisuretime70; 10b Aleksandar Mirkovic; 11c Yulan; 11c Sophy Kozlova; fccr, 11br Ffatserifade; 13tr PepeLaguarda/iStockphoto.com; fcbr, 13b Andreykuzmin; 15c Artcomedy; 15tr Grafistart; 16r Andresr; 17br Valeriy Kachaev; 18c 79mtk; fctc, 19b Witr; bcc, 20bl, Dedmazay; fcbl, 20c, 30tr Nikolais; 22c NASA; 23tr Gstudioimagen; 23b NASA; 24c, 30b Snicol24; fctc, 24b Theblackrhino; fctr, 25tr Deomister; 25c Photozirka; 25cr Radu191289; 25bl Thumeau; 26c Skillividden; 27t Gbuglok; 27c drmakkoy/iStockphoto.com; 28c misterspike; 28b Zygotehasnobrain; 29t Winnond; 29b Mycoolsites; 32t Stylephotographs

Teaching Guide

Visit this Scholastic Web site to download the Teaching Guide for this series:
www.factsfornow.scholastic.com
Enter the keywords **Get In Shape**

MIX
Paper from
responsible sources
FSC® C104740

Contents

Flat Shapes   4

Triangles   6

Right **Triangles**   8

Changing Shapes   10

Tiling   12

Round and **Round**   14

Solids   16

Prisms and **Pyramids**   18

Flattening **Solids**   20

Spheres   22

Cylinders, Cones, and **Toruses**   24

Size **Matters**   26

Quiz   28

Glossary   31

Index, Facts for Now, and Answers   32

Flat Shapes

We use a kind of math called geometry to describe the shapes we see around us. We define the shapes by their properties. The simplest shapes are those with two dimensions, which we can draw on a piece of paper. They have an area but do not have a depth.

Polygons

Shapes with straight sides are called polygons. Regular polygons have sides of equal length and equal interior angles. All regular polygons can fit exactly inside a circle. Each interior angle is always less than 180°, but the more sides the shape has, the closer the angles get to 180°, and the tighter it fits inside its circle.

A **regular triangle** (also called an equilateral triangle) has **three sides** and an interior angle of **60°**.

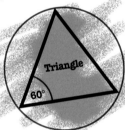

A **square** has **four sides** and an interior angle of **90°**.

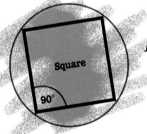

A **regular octagon** has **eight sides** and an interior angle of **135°**.

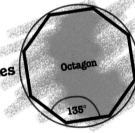

A **regular octadecagon** has **18 sides** and an interior angle of **160°**.

A regular polygon with **1 million sides** is called a **megagon**. It has interior angles of **179.9996°**. To the naked eye, it would look like a circle.

Symmetry

A shape is symmetrical if it can be flipped or turned to make the same shape.

Reflection

With reflection symmetry, one half of a shape is the reflection, or "mirror image," of another. The faces of many animals show reflection symmetry—the left side is a mirror image of the right.

Rotation

If a shape can be rotated around its center and stay the same, it has rotational symmetry. A sea star has rotational symmetry if it is rotated around an angle of 72°.

72°

Backyard Fence

HOUSE THIS SIDE

8 feet

6 feet

The perimeter of a shape is the total length of its sides. If you are buying fencing for a backyard, you need to know the perimeter of your yard.

Sarah has a rectangular yard that is 6 feet wide and 8 feet long. If fencing is sold in 2-foot sections, how much fencing will Sarah need to buy?

For Sarah to solve her problem, she needs to know the perimeter of the yard minus the side that faces the house. This leaves just three sides to be fenced in. So Sarah needs

8 + 6 + 8 feet
of fencing, which is
22 feet, or 11 sections.

Triangles

A three-sided polygon is called a triangle. Triangles can be described in terms of the length of their sides or the size of their angles.

What Type of Angle?

Equilateral triangles have **equal sides** and **equal angles.**

If you stand straight, with your legs apart, you are making an **isosceles triangle** with your legs. Isosceles triangles have **two equal sides** and **two equal angles**. They form a strong shape when you stand because an equal weight is pushed onto each leg.

An **acute triangle** is a triangle whose angles are **all less than 90°**.

A **right triangle** is a triangle with **one angle that is exactly 90°** (known as a right angle).

An **obtuse triangle** has **one angle** that is **greater than 90°**.

Isosceles

75°   75°

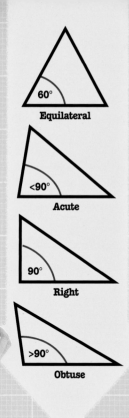

60°
Equilateral

<90°
Acute

90°
Right

>90°
Obtuse

The Area of a Triangle

If you multiply the **height** of a triangle by its **base**, you get the **area** of a rectangle that the triangle sits inside. The area of the triangle is equal to ½ **of the area** of this rectangle.

The equation for the area looks like this:

Area = hb/2

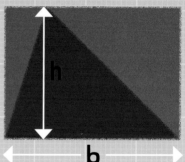

The Adding of Angles

Draw a **triangle** on a piece of paper, then cut off the **three corners** and fit them around **a single point**. The three angles fitted together will make a straight line. You can try this with any triangle, and the result will be the same. This is a property of triangles— the three internal angles always **add up to 180°**.

Scalene triangles have no equal sides and no equal angles.

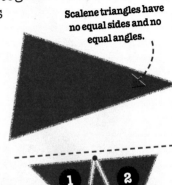

Architects use isosceles triangles when building bridges. The shape makes the structure very strong by distributing the weight evenly.

All triangles have three internal angles that add up to 180°.
This comes in very handy for mathematicians.

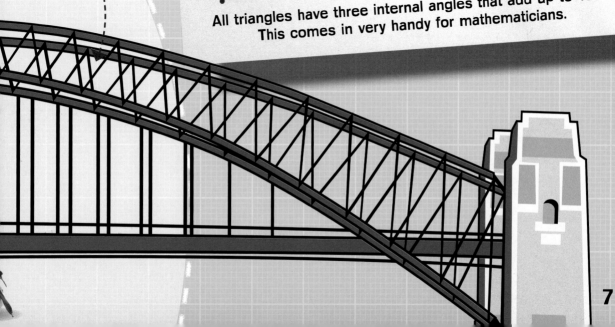

Right Triangles

Right triangles have one 90° angle. They have special properties that make them extremely useful in solving many kinds of problems.

PITAGORA

The Pythagorean Theorem

Around 2,500 years ago, the Greek mathematician Pythagoras discovered an amazing fact about right triangles. Now known as the Pythagorean theorem, it states that:

The square of the hypotenuse is equal to the sum of the squares of the other two sides.

The hypotenuse is the side of the triangle opposite the right angle.

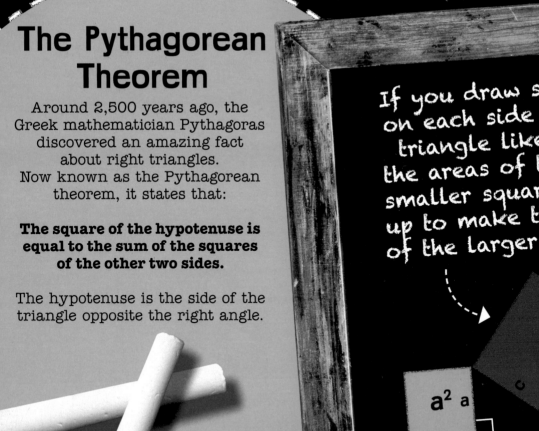

If you draw squares on each side of the triangle like this, the areas of the two smaller squares add up to make the area of the larger square.

c^2

c

a^2 a

b

b^2

Pythagorean Triples

Pythagorean triples are special right triangles that have sides with lengths that are whole numbers.

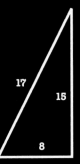 

You can use a 3, 4, 5 right triangle to check whether the corners on a carpet are right angles. Measure 30 inches along one side of the carpet, and 40 inches along the other side. If the diagonal is 50 inches long, the corner must be a right angle. If it is more than 50 inches, the corner is an obtuse angle. If it is less than 50 inches, the corner is an acute angle.

30 in

40 in

?? in

a^2

b^2

c^2

To see that this is true, take four identical right triangles and arrange them so that the four right angles become the four corners of a square (you can do this with any right triangle):

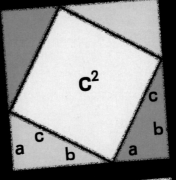

Now rearrange the four triangles like so:

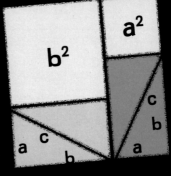

In the first diagram, the triangles form a square with c^2. In the second diagram, they form the same square with a^2 and b^2. Therefore

$$a^2 + b^2 = c^2$$

Changing Shapes

A transformation is a way of changing a shape according to a set of mathematical rules.

Stretching Shapes

Shapes can be distorted by transformations. A shear fixes points on one line, but shifts all other points to one side.

A stretch fixes points on one line, but moves all other points up or down.

Translation

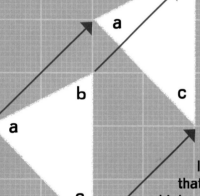

A translation moves a shape from one place to another without changing its appearance. Each corner moves exactly the same distance and in the same direction.

Here, the shape of a tree has been translated exactly, but within a field of perspective lines. It is an optical illusion that tricks us into believing that the higher image is farther away. Because we think it's farther away, our brains tell us that it is bigger. Check for yourself with a ruler—both trees are exactly the same size!

un house mirrors are curved in a way that shears and stretches the reflected image.

Reflection

A reflection produces a "mirror image" of a shape. Each point on the shape is moved so that it is the same distance away from the mirror line but on the opposite side.

Resizing

Resizing makes a shape bigger or smaller. The change in size is described by a scale factor. For example, a scale factor of 3 will make each side of a shape 3 times as long. A scale factor of ⅓ will make each side one-third of the length. The shapes look similar because they have the same internal angles.

Maps use really small scale factors to represent areas that may be many miles across. This map has a scale factor of 1:100,000, meaning that 1 mile on the ground is represented by just 1 inch on the map.

"It's on the left, right?"

0   0.5   1 mi

"What?!!"

Tiling

Tiling, or tessellation, is the fitting together of shapes in a way that leaves no gaps between them.

Regular Tessellation

Regular tessellation is tiling using just one regular shape. Only regular shapes with interior angles that divide into 360 can tessellate, as they need to be able to fit exactly around one point. This means that there are just three possibilities:

Squares

A square has angles of 90°, meaning that four squares can fit around a point.

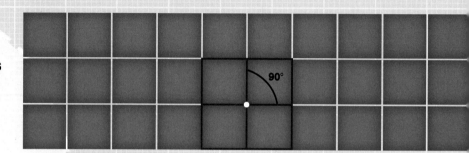

Equilateral Triangles

An equilateral triangle has angles of 60°, meaning that six equilateral triangles can fit around a point.

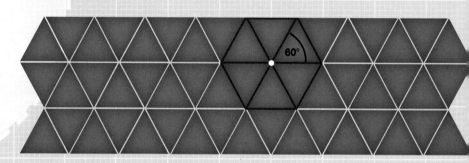

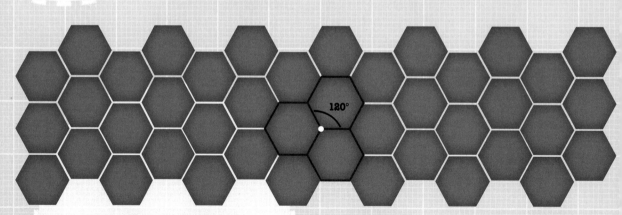

Regular Hexagons

A regular hexagon has angles of 120°, meaning that three can fit around a point.

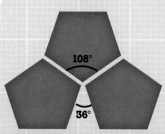

Regular tessellation won't work with any other shape. For example, a pentagon (left) has internal angles of 108°. This does not divide into 360°.

Semi-regular Tessellations

You can combine two different regular polygons to make tessellations. In semi-regular tessellations, the number of sides touching at each vertex (corner) is the same.

The combination above is a semi-regular tessellation of hexagons and triangles.

Islamic Art

Beautiful tessellated patterns are a common feature in Islamic art. Islamic artists cover walls with self-repeating patterns that could go on forever. Can you see the reflection and rotation symmetry in this design?

Bees are experts at tiling. They construct their honeycombs using regular hexagons.

Round and Round

A circle is a shape made from a line of points that are the same distance from another point. That point becomes the center of the circle. We can draw a circle using a compass. One arm of the compass stays at the center while the other draws the circle.

The distance from the center to the edge of a circle is called the radius. Twice that distance gives the diameter. The distance around the outside of the circle is its circumference.

radius (r)

circumference

Pi

Once you know the radius (**r**) of a circle, you can work out its area and circumference using a special number called π or pi. Pi is the number you get when you divide a circle's circumference (**c**) by its diameter (**d**).

$$\pi = c/d \text{ or } \pi = c/2r$$

This gives the equation $c = 2\pi r$ for the circumference of a circle. The area of a circle is equal to πr^2

Pi is a special number that goes on forever when it is written out. Here's how it starts: 3.14159265358979323846264338327950 28841971693993751058209749445923078164062862089986 28 03482534211706798214808651328230664709384460955058 22

How Much Pizza?

A section of a circle made by two radiuses is called a sector. A slice of pizza is a sector of the whole pizza. The angle between the radiuses determines the number of slices. This angle is equal to 360° divided by the number of slices.

Here, there are eight slices of pizza, meaning that the angle between the radiuses is 45°.

diameter (d)

45°

sector

Darts

A dartboard is a circle divided into 20 sectors. The angle between each radius is equal to 18°.

18°

Ellipses

An ellipse is an oval that looks like a squashed circle.

Unlike a circle, an ellipse does not have a center. Instead, it has two points called its focuses. The sum of the distances from any point on the ellipse to both focuses is always the same.

$$a + b = c + d$$

Solar System

The orbits of the planets around the sun are ellipses, with the sun at one of the two focuses.

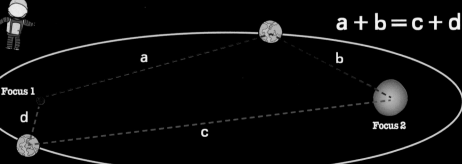

a

b

Focus 1

d

c

Focus 2

Solids

So far we have been dealing with shapes in two dimensions. Shapes in three dimensions are called solids.

Polyhedrons

Solids with flat faces are called polyhedrons (meaning "many faces").

Before it is inflated, a soccer ball is an example of a polyhedron. It is made from a combination of **pentagons** and **hexagons**.

Hexagon

Pentagon

When the soccer ball is filled with air, it turns into a **sphere**. A sphere does not have flat faces, and is called a non-polyhedron solid.

Regular Solids

"Wow, I'm full of hot air!"

There are five regular solids, known as the Platonic solids. They are named after the ancient Greek philosopher Plato, who was one of the first to describe them. Each face of a Platonic solid is the same shape, and each vertex has the same angle.

Tetrahedron
four faces, each
a triangle

Cube
six faces,
each a square

Octahedron
eight faces, each
a triangle

Dodecahedron
twelve faces, each
a pentagon

Icosahedron
twenty faces, each
a triangle

An Impossible Shape!

Mathematicians love to play around with 3-D shapes and come up with 2-D drawings of solids that are impossible to make. The British mathematician Roger Penrose invented the Penrose triangle. Can you see why it would be impossible to make one?

Fair Dice

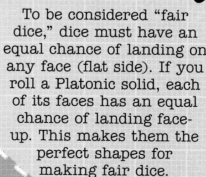

To be considered "fair dice," dice must have an equal chance of landing on any face (flat side). If you roll a Platonic solid, each of its faces has an equal chance of landing face-up. This makes them the perfect shapes for making fair dice.

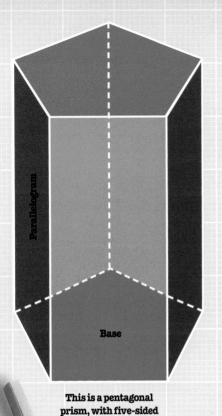

Parallelogram

Base

This is a pentagonal prism, with five-sided pentagons at the bases.

Prisms and Pyramids

Prisms

A prism is a solid with two ends, or bases, that are the same shape, parallel, and connected to each other by straight lines. The shape of the base gives the prism its name. The sides are parallelograms—four-sided shapes with two pairs of parallel sides.

Volume of a Prism

A prism's volume (V) is the area of its base (A) × its length (L): $V = A \times L$

Right Prisms

A right prism is a prism with rectangles along its sides. An Allen wrench (left) is the shape of a right prism with a 90° bend in it.

Irregular Prisms

Irregular prisms have bases with irregular polygons. Houses are often the shape of an irregular right prism, with the base on the side of the house.

"This isn't my good side."

Base

Pyramids

A pyramid has a flat polygon base. Each side of the pyramid is a triangle. The sides meet at a point called the apex.

A pyramid is named after the shape of its base. This is a pentagonal pyramid.

A pentagonal pyramid has:

6 faces
(including the base)

5 triangular sides

6 corners
(including the apex)

10 edges

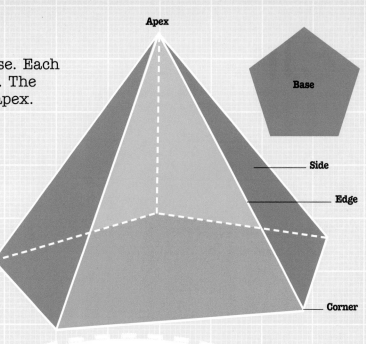

Apex

Base

Side

Edge

Corner

Pyramids at Giza

The three pyramids at Giza in Egypt are square pyramids. The largest and oldest was built more than 4,500 years ago as a tomb for the pharaoh Khufu. It was the world's tallest building for nearly 4,000 years. The pyramid is made of more than 2 million stone blocks weighing an average of 2.8 tons each. The pyramids are carefully positioned so that their four corners face north, south, east, and west.

Flattening Solids

If you unfold a solid into a flat shape, you produce a net. There may be several different ways to make a net from one kind of solid.

Net of a Cube

The simplest way to unfold a cube is probably net number 4, but a cube can also be unfolded into 10 other nets.

All 11 of these nets can make a cube with a lid that opens like a jack-in-the-box.

Do you see how each net can be folded into a cube?

Finding Surface Areas

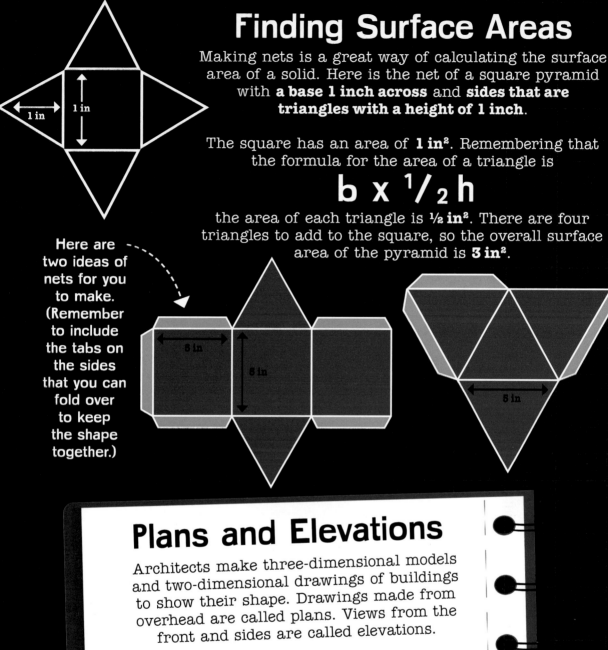

Making nets is a great way of calculating the surface area of a solid. Here is the net of a square pyramid with **a base 1 inch across** and **sides that are triangles with a height of 1 inch**.

The square has an area of **1 in²**. Remembering that the formula for the area of a triangle is

$$b \times {}^1\!/_2\,h$$

the area of each triangle is **½ in²**. There are four triangles to add to the square, so the overall surface area of the pyramid is **3 in²**.

Here are two ideas of nets for you to make. (Remember to include the tabs on the sides that you can fold over to keep the shape together.)

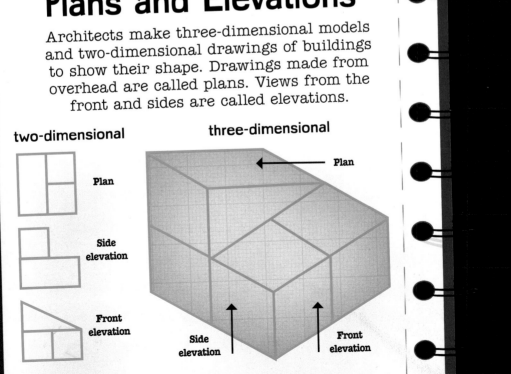

Plans and Elevations

Architects make three-dimensional models and two-dimensional drawings of buildings to show their shape. Drawings made from overhead are called plans. Views from the front and sides are called elevations.

two-dimensional

Plan

Side elevation

Front elevation

three-dimensional

Plan

Side elevation

Front elevation

Spheres

A sphere is a solid on which all points on the surface are the same distance from the center. A sphere is perfectly symmetrical and has no edges or corners.

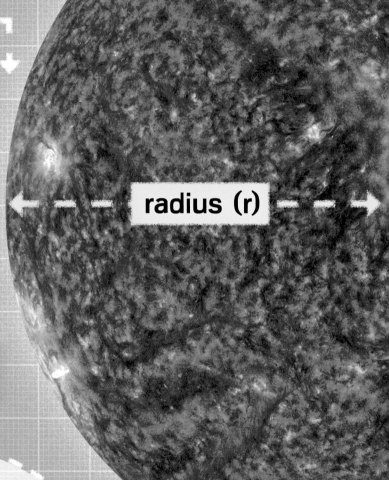

Volume and Surface Area

We need the special number pi (see page 14) to work out a sphere's surface area and volume. These are the equations:

Surface area =
$$4\pi r^2$$

radius (r)

Volume =
$$\tfrac{4}{3}\pi r^3$$

Spheres in Nature

A sphere has a special quality: it is the shape with the maximum volume for the minimum surface area. For this reason, spheres appear in lots of places in nature where forces squeeze matter together, from stars and planets to raindrops.

Raindrops

High in the sky, raindrops form as tiny spheres of water. As they fall to the ground, the spheres become squashed at the bottom because the air pressure is greater at the bottom than at the top. If the drops become too big, they break apart to form smaller spheres.

The Sun and Earth

The most perfect natural sphere around us is the sun. The sun has a radius of

435,000 miles.

It has a tiny bulge at the equator, meaning that it is 6 miles wider at its equator than from pole to pole. If scaled down to the size of a beach ball, that difference would be less than the width of a human hair.

Equator

Like the sun, Earth is also slightly squashed at the equator. This squashed shape is called an oblate spheroid.

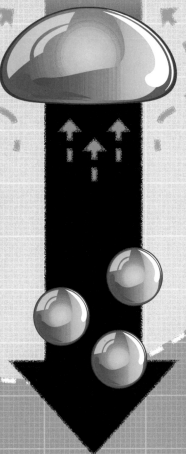

23

Circular end

Curved side

Cylinders, Cones, and Toruses

Cylinders

A cylinder is a solid with flat, circular ends connected by one curved side. Like a prism (page 18), the cross-section of a cylinder is the same wherever you cut it.

A cake is the shape of a cylinder. To work out the **volume** of a cake (assuming it has the same thickness all the way through), you multiply the area of the circular base by its height (h), or thickness. **Volume =**

$$\pi \times r^2 \times h$$

The **surface area** of a cylinder is the circumference of the circle × its height, plus the areas of the circular top and bottom. **Surface area =**

$$2\pi rh + 2\pi r^2$$

radius (r)

height (h)

Soda cans are shaped as cylinders to make the packaging more efficient. A circle is the shape with the maximum area for its circumference, so more liquid can be held in a cylindrical can than one shaped like a prism. The most efficient packaging would be a sphere, but spherical cans would roll off the shelves!

Cones

A cone is a solid with a **circular base** and one curved side ending in a point called its apex.

You can make a cone by rotating a right triangle (in red) around its right angle.

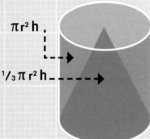

Side length

Height

$\pi r^2 h$

$\frac{1}{3}\pi r^2 h$

Radius

The formula for the volume of a cone is similar to that of a cylinder.

Volume =

$$\frac{1}{3}\pi \times r^2 \times h$$

This means that the volume of a cone that fits tightly inside a cylinder is exactly one-third the volume of the cylinder.

Mount Fuji in Japan is a volcano. Its cone-shaped slopes have been formed from molten lava flowing out in all directions during eruptions.

Torus

A torus is a ring-shaped solid. It is made by rotating a circle around a circular axis.

A torus made with a large circle looks like a doughnut. With a smaller circle, it looks more like a bicycle tire.

axis

Size Matters

Why Are Polar Bears So Big?

A problem faced by all animals that live in the icy polar regions is how to keep warm. A polar bear has thick fur, but its huge size also helps it conserve heat. We lose heat through our skin, so to stay warm, we want to have as small a surface area relative to our mass as possible. To see how a polar bear's huge size helps it keep warm, look at what happens when you scale up a sphere.

Using the formulas on page 22, the smaller sphere (**a**) has a volume of $4/3\pi$

It has a surface area of 4π

This means that its **surface area** is **three times greater than its volume**.

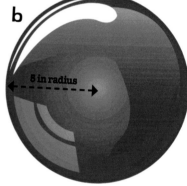

b

5 in radius

a

1 in radius

The larger sphere (**b**) has a volume of

$500/3\pi$

and a surface area of

100π

Its **volume** is **1.6 times greater than its surface area**. Volume increases by a cube of the scaling factor, but surface area only increases by a square of the scaling factor. If you want to keep warm in the Arctic, it pays to be big!

"So that's why I'm big-boned!"

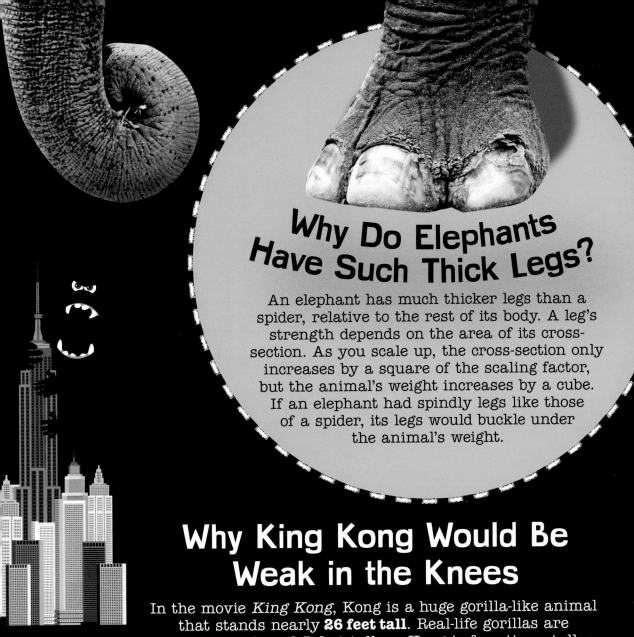

Why Do Elephants Have Such Thick Legs?

An elephant has much thicker legs than a spider, relative to the rest of its body. A leg's strength depends on the area of its cross-section. As you scale up, the cross-section only increases by a square of the scaling factor, but the animal's weight increases by a cube. If an elephant had spindly legs like those of a spider, its legs would buckle under the animal's weight.

Why King Kong Would Be Weak in the Knees

In the movie *King Kong*, Kong is a huge gorilla-like animal that stands nearly **26 feet tall**. Real-life gorillas are never more than 6.5 feet tall, so Kong is four times taller than a gorilla, but with the same relative dimensions to his body, head, and legs.

A large gorilla weighs about **440 pounds,** and its leg bones have a cross-section area of about **4 in^2**. Standing on two legs, that means **440 pounds** supported by **8 in^2**, which makes **55 pounds per in^2**.

King Kong would weigh **440 pounds** × **4^3**, which is **28,160 pounds**. His leg bones would have a cross-section area of **10 × 2.5 in^2**, which is **25 in^2**. Standing on two legs, **28,160 pounds** would be supported by **50 in^2**, which makes **563 pounds per in^2**, or about 123 pounds more than the average gorilla weighs. Kong would have struggled to stand up, let alone climb the Empire State Building!

Quiz

3 Use **Pythagoras's theorem** to work out the **value of c.**

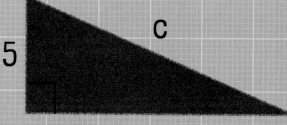

C

5

12

1 How do you fit one hexagon together with three equilateral triangles to make

one equilateral triangle?

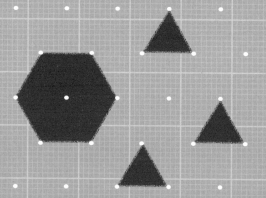

4 Face A has been **resized** to make face B. What was the **scale factor** used?

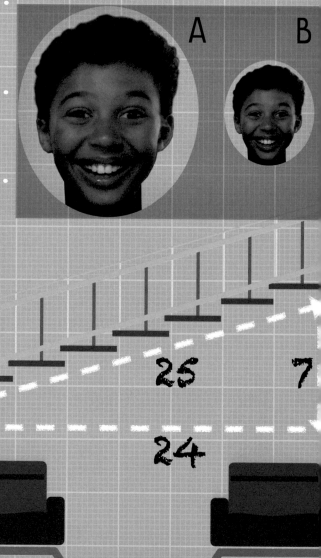

A

B

2 Use **Pythagoras's theorem** to work out whether this staircase is a

right triangle.

25

7

24

5 Look at the following **tessellations** of hexagons and triangles. Which pattern is **not semi-regular?**

a)

b)

c)

7 This wheel has a **diameter** of 8 inches. What is the **area** of the wheel?

8 Which three **Platonic solids** can be made using **triangles?**

9 What **shape** would you use to make a fair die with the **numbers 1 to 12** written on its faces?

6 You have one pizza that you want to share equally among **eight people**. If you slice the pizza into eight pieces, what will be the angle **between each radius?**

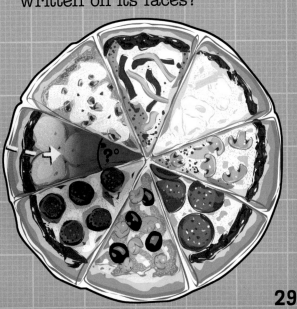

10 What is the **volume** of this **prism**?

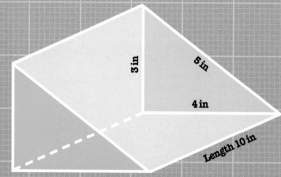

3 in
5 in
4 in
Length 10 in

11 This is a **hexagonal** pyramid.

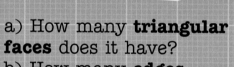

a) How many **triangular faces** does it have?
b) How many **edges** does it have?

12 Which of the following is a **net of a cube?**

a)

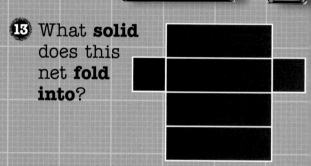

b)

c)

13 What **solid** does this net **fold into?**

14 This cake has a **diameter** of 8 inches and a thickness of 2 inches. Use a calculator and the value of 3.14 for π to work out its **volume**.

diameter

height

Glossary

Acute angle
An angle that is less than 90°.

Cross-section
A shape that is made by cutting through a solid.

Equator
An imaginary line around Earth. The equator forms a circle that is the same distance from the North and South Poles. It is 24,900 miles long.

Geometry
The branch of mathematics that deals with points, lines, shapes, solids, and dimensions.

Hypotenuse
The side of a right triangle that is opposite the right angle. The hypotenuse is always the longest side of a right triangle.

Obtuse angle
An angle that is more than 90° but less than 180°.

Pi (π)
The number produced by dividing the circumference of a circle by its diameter. Pi equals about 3.14, but it is impossible to write it down exactly.

Platonic solids
The five regular solids. They have faces made of regular polygons, and the same number of faces meet at each vertex, or corner.

Polygon
A two-dimensional shape made with straight lines.

Polyhedron
A three-dimensional solid made by joining together polygons.

Right angle
An angle equal to 90°. A right angle is exactly one-quarter of a full turn.

Scale factor
The ratio of the length of an object in a drawing or model to the length of the real thing. With a scale factor of 1:100, 1 inch in a drawing would represent 100 inches in the original.

Symmetry
Agreement in size, shape, and relative position of parts on opposite sides of a line or around a central point.

Tessellation
An arrangement of shapes to cover a surface without leaving gaps or overlapping. Also called tiling.

Transformation
A way of changing a shape using mathematical rules. A transformation may move the shape from one place to another, change its size, or alter its shape by stretching or squashing it.

Translation
A transformation that moves a shape from one place to another.

Index

acute triangle 6
Allen wrench 18
apex 25

bees 13

circles 14–15
circumference 14
compass 15
cones 25
cube 17, 20
cylinders 24

dartboard 15
diameter 14
dice 17
dodecahedron 17
doughnut 25

Earth 23
elephant 27
elevations 21
ellipse 15
equator 23
equilateral triangles
    4, 6, 12

focus 15
Fuji, Mount 25
fun house mirrors 11

geometry 4
Giza, pyramids at 19

hexagon 12, 16

honeycombs 13
hypotenuse 8

icosahedron 17
Islamic art 13
isosceles triangle 6

Khufu 19
King Kong 27

maps 11
megagon 4

nets 20–21

oblate spheroid 23
obtuse triangle 6
octadecagon 4
octagon 4
octahedron 17
optical illusion 10
Penrose, Roger 17

pentagon 12, 16
perimeter 5
pi (π) 14, 22
pizza 14–15
plans 21
Platonic solids 17
polar bears 26
polygons 4, 6
polyhedrons 16
prisms 18
pyramids 19, 21

Pythagoras 8
Pythagorean triples 9

radius 14–15, 22
raindrops 23
reflection 5, 11
resizing 11
right triangle 7, 8–9
rotation 5

scale factor 11
scalene triangle 7
sea star 5
sector 15
semi-regular tessellation 13
shear 10
solids 16–17, 20–21
spheres 22–23
spheroid 23
square 4, 12
stretch 10
sun 23
symmetry 5

tessellation 12–13
tetrahedron 17
tiling 12–13
tire 25
toruses 25
transformations 10–11
translation 10
triangles 4, 6–7, 8–9, 12

Facts for Now

Visit this Scholastic Web site for more information
on shapes and to download the
Teaching Guide for this series:
www.factsfornow.scholastic.com
Enter the keywords **Get In Shape**

Answers

1.

2. $7^2 + 24^2 = 49 + 576 = 625 = 25^2$. It is a right triangle.

3. $c^2 = 5^2 + 12^2 = 25 + 144 = 169$. So $c = 13$

4. Scale factor ½

5. c is not semi-regular. The vertices are not all the same.

6. $360° ÷ 8 = 45°$

7. Area $= π × 4^2 = 3.14 × 16 = 50.24$ in²

8. Tetrahedron, octahedron, icosahedron

9. A dodecahedron

10. The area of the base is 6 in². Volume is 6 in² × 10 in = 60 in³

11. a) 6 b) 12

12. c is a net of a cube

13. It is a square prism

14. $π × 4^2 × 2 = 32π = 100$ in³